CHANGE
YOUR ROOM

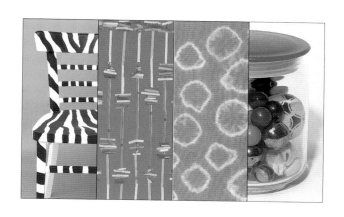

CHANGE
YOUR ROOM

JANE BULL

DORLING KINDERSLEY
LONDON • NEW YORK • SYDNEY • MOSCOW
www.dk.com

A DORLING KINDERSLEY BOOK
www.dk.com

for Charlotte, Billy, and James

DESIGN • Jane Bull
TEXT • Caroline Greene
PHOTOGRAPHY • Andy Crawford

EDITORS • Penny Smith, Sue Leonard
DTP DESIGNERS • Almudena Díaz, Heather McCarry
MANAGING ART EDITOR • Rachael Foster
MANAGING EDITOR • Mary Ling
PRODUCTION • Lisa Moss

MODELS • Charlotte Bull, Tom Greene,
Michaela Paul-Smith, Chetna Kapacee

Published in Great Britain
by Dorling Kindersley Limited
9 Henrietta Street, London WC2E 8PS
2 4 6 8 10 9 7 5 3 1

A CIP catalogue record for this book
is available from the British Library

ISBN: 0-7513-5949-1

Colour reproduction by GRB Editrice s.r.l., Verona, Italy
Printed and bound in Italy by L.E.G.O.

Contents

Introduction

Changing your room may be easier than you think, especially if you have a few ideas of your own. Just remember that not everyone has a handy carpenter around or a resident interior decorator. So it helps to be realistic about what you are going to be able to manage. For a start, give your things a good sort out. You'll have to be tough and decide: does it stay? Or does it go? Next be bold and change the furniture around and see your room from a new perspective. Now for the decorating. Ideas about colour and images can come from objects around you, so many projects in this book are based on creating an original look for yourself out of the things you already have. All you have to do now is set to work and enjoy yourself!

Jane Bull.

1 Time for a CHANGE

Plan of ACTION

Before you start giving your room a new look, it helps to be able to visualize some of the changes. Making a plan of your room gets you started. It lets you see how practical your ideas are, especially if you want to move your furniture around. With a 3-D model, you can even experiment with colour using small sample pots of paint.

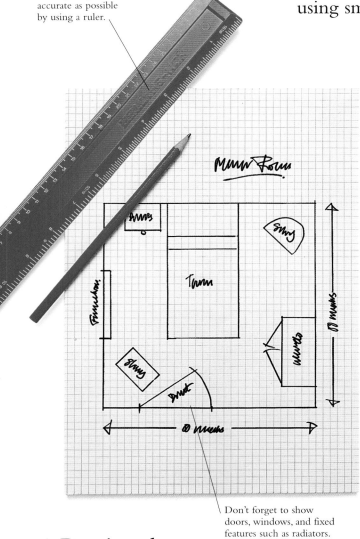

Make your plan as accurate as possible by using a ruler.

Don't forget to show doors, windows, and fixed features such as radiators.

▲ Drawing plans

Write down the exact measurements of all the walls in your room, including any awkward angles. Then draw a diagram of your room using graph paper to keep it to scale (e.g. 1 square = 10 cm).

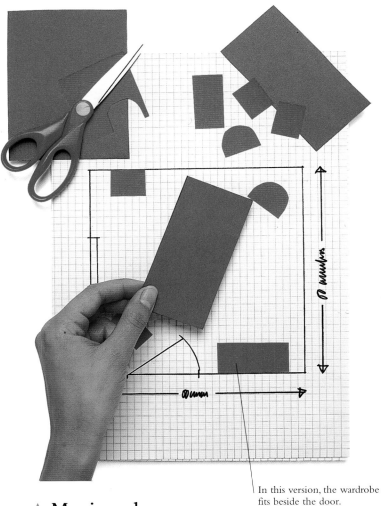

In this version, the wardrobe fits beside the door.

▲ Moving plans

When you've drawn the plan, cut out pieces of paper to represent the furniture and any other movable items in your room. Then you can shift them around the plan to see how they fit into different places in the room.

3-D plan ▶

A three-dimensional model will help you visualize more strongly how your room will look once you've moved the furniture around. You can make a model with doll's-house furniture and even try out a colour scheme. The mini room set may help convince you – and your family – that the change is a good idea.

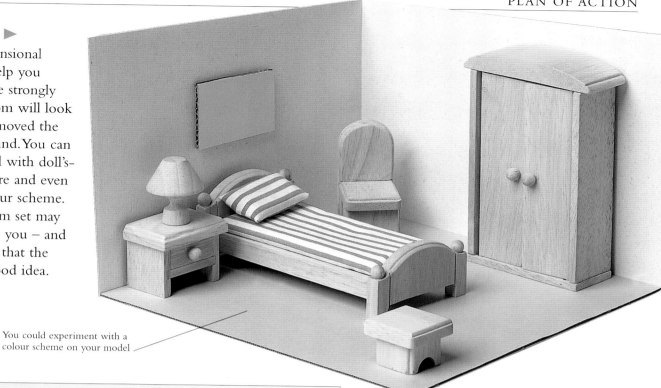

You could experiment with a colour scheme on your model

◀ Elements to decorate

You can transform your room just by changing things that no one minds you decorating. An old chair or chest of drawers may be crying out for a makeover. By sorting your stuff and decorating old boxes you can improve storage. Then there are lampshades and cushions to decorate.

▲ Planning colour

You may already know what colours you want to use, but swatch samples are helpful when you're choosing a scheme.

COLOUR Changes

Colour is the key to creating a new look, whatever furniture your room contains. Whether you have a favourite colour you want to keep, or a new shade you're longing to try, the colour wheel helps draw it all together.

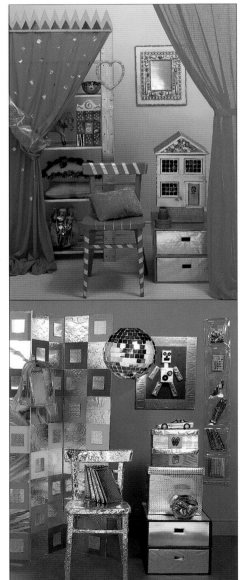

1
Harmonious hues

This scheme uses colours from the same side of the colour wheel, ranging here from scarlet to purple. Use colours from other parts of the wheel for an intense, co-ordinated effect.

2
Silver spectrum

Draw on all the colours of the spectrum by using elements from all round the colour wheel. Blue, red, purple, yellow, and green are reflected in silver foil, plastics, and holographic papers.

Primary colours
These are RED, BLUE, YELLOW. They are found on opposite sides of the colour wheel.

Secondary colours
These are GREEN, ORANGE, PURPLE. They are formed from a mixture of two primary colours: blue + yellow = green, red + yellow = orange, red + blue = purple. Secondary colours are found between the primaries on the colour wheel.

RED

BLUE

Making a colour wheel

Make your own colour wheel by collecting swatches of paint colours from DIY stores. Cut the swatches up, then arrange them in order of the colours of the spectrum (red, orange, yellow, green, blue, purple), and glue them to the rim of a paper plate. Now you have a handy tool to help you pick colours for your scheme.

Harmonious colours

These are next to one another on the wheel and are from similar colour ranges such as all the warm red hues.

Complementary colours

These are any colours from opposite sides of the wheel. They contrast with one another.

YELLOW

3
Wild contrasts

Black and white, and colours from opposite sides of the wheel produce striking contrasts. Here zebra patterns are offset by orange and its opposites blue and green.

4
Sunshine shades

These colours are next to each other on the wheel, spanning a range that gives an outdoor summertime feel. Blues and greens, dominated by yellow, convey a sense of space and sunshine.

5
Comic colours

The bold primary colours of red, blue, and yellow are contrasted by the secondary colour of the green background. Inspiration comes from cartoons, comics, and computer games.

1 Harmonious HUES

Ideas for the kind of decoration you want can come from something as simple as a collection of buttons.

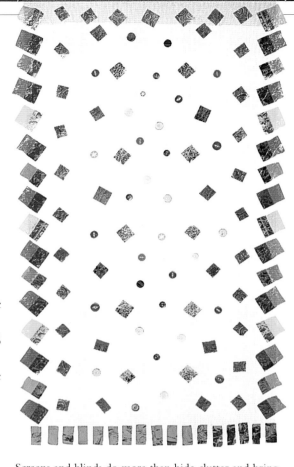

This scheme uses colours from the same side of the colour wheel, bringing together shades and tones of pink, highlighted with gold. You can apply the same principle using blues, greens, or yellows.

Screens and blinds do more than hide clutter and bring privacy – they add colour and sparkle to windows and shelves. For this blind, simple transparent material is decorated with buttons, foil, and sweet wrappers (see p. 79).

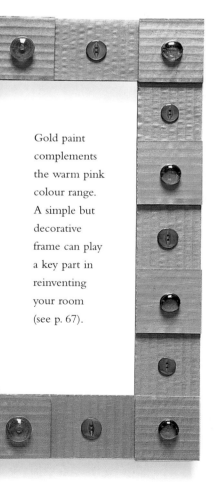

Gold paint complements the warm pink colour range. A simple but decorative frame can play a key part in reinventing your room (see p. 67).

Decorative elements such as ribbons or fake fur add texture to the colour scheme.

Buttons or glass beads enrich doorknobs and drawer handles (see p. 62).

14

Shelving

Disguise your shelves or cupboards with a screen (see opposite) or length of fabric that can simply be pinned up with thumbtacks. Make a top border for the shelves with cardboard and metallic paper.

Frames

Posters, photographs, or mirrors can all be livened up with frames made from cardboard, and odds and ends (see p. 64). Try to match a frame to the subject of the picture.

Make your own

You can make any number of decorative objects to create your new look. Pots (see p. 84), cushion covers (see p. 72), and collection boxes (see p. 90) all add to the display.

Simple storage

Not all favourite toys have to be thrown out once you've outgrown them. The doll's-house here is painted to match the colour scheme, and can be used to store all kinds of bits and pieces.

Chairs

Paint your chair a bold basic colour from your scheme and add detail in a contrasting colour or texture – gold ribbon as here, or a feather boa (see p. 57).

2 Silver SPECTRUM

A simple frame made from card and covered in foil brings strong lines to your walls. Decorate the border by scoring a pattern in the foil using a blunt pencil.

Glue spare nuts and bolts to your door handle for a mechanical touch (see p. 63).

Metallic materials and square lines dominate this spacey, shiny effect. The whole spectrum of colours is reflected in the foil as bold screen panels bring more light into the room.

To make a glitter ball, first find a round paper lampshade. Cut up small squares of sticky-backed mirror card and stick them to the lampshade. Work around the shade to get even rows of little mirrors. Hang the ball from the ceiling, but don't use it as a lampshade since the card may unstick from the heat of a bulb.

Art shops and stationers sell a wide range of reflective card and paper.

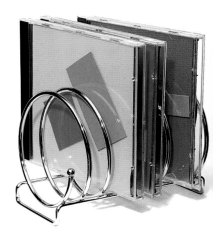

A wire toast rack found in a market makes a good CD holder and is a useful storage solution (see p. 33).

Screens

This screen is simply an old one that's been covered in large sheets of foil. It is decorated with colourful frames around reflective card. You can make your own screen using panels of cardboard.

Glitter ball

This is not a lampshade but a great sparkling ball that reflects light from its hundreds of tiny mirrors. It acts as a strong focus in any room (see opposite).

Frames

Framed pictures or mirrors transform your walls (p. 64). For an added dimension you can make your own 3-D collage from small foil-covered boxes.

Storage

Boxes of all sizes can be recycled to make handy storage containers. Just cover them with paper and add a contents motif. Plastic pockets are also useful (see pp. 26–7).

Chairs

Re-upholster your chair with kitchen foil that's scrunched into shape and taped down (see p. 57). It's cheap, and easy to repair as well.

3 Wild CONTRASTS

To copy any animal design, it is a good idea to use clear animal pictures and try out a few patterns on rough paper first.

Your redecorated room should help you keep things tidy: hanging up clothes doesn't need to be boring (see p. 88).

Once you've decided on your colours, make sure you are choosing the right type of paint (see p. 42).

Contrasting colours make bold patterns, so let nature be your guide, and experiment with animal prints and jungle colours. Or simply decorate your room with strong geometric patterns.

Give your collections a new lease of life by lining them up in an interesting or funny way (see p. 36).

Papier-mâché pots are easy to make and can echo other design ideas in your room (see p. 84).

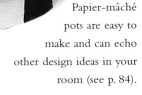

Shelves and screens

Transform your shelves by painting them and adding a strip of bold calico. Pin tapes to the top of the shelves, roll up the blind, and hold in place with bows.

Lampshades

You can complement the other patterns in your room by making a paper shade that covers an existing lampshade or ceiling light (see p. 80).

Frames

Whether you are putting up a mask or a poster, a customized frame looks great. You can paint it, or cover it with fake fur or an animal collage (see p. 64).

Storage

Boxes of all sizes (see p. 26 and p. 90) make cheap and useful storage – and a rope ladder may be more useful inside than out!

Chairs

With a design like this, your chair will become your own four-legged friend (see p. 54). Cushions add a soft touch (see p. 72).

4 Sunshine SHADES

For decoration use stickers or cut-outs from magazines.

With blues, greens, yellows, and highlights of **orange**, a rainy day will never get you down when your room is full of **nature's** brightest colours.

Plain furniture can be reborn with a pattern of whirls and waves. If you want to echo a different theme, try animal prints, a collage, or rich golden relief (see p. 58).

Bring the outdoors indoors by covering a chair with summer flowers and butterflies (see p. 54).

Stencils make simple patterns for walls, drawers, or cupboard doors (see p. 53).

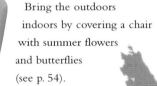

What's bugging you? This doorknob is a good way of saying "Keep out!" (see p. 62).

Shelves and screens

These shelves make a colourful frame for a simple muslin curtain. Pin lengths of string from the top of the shelves, roll up the fabric, and tie it in place with bows.

Frames

Make your own summery frame (see p. 67) and then mount it on a sheet of painted cardboard for a more striking effect.

Cushions

Put pictures on cushions with shapes cut out of material and sewn onto plain covers. Here the cactus is made from face-cloths (see p. 75).

Simple storage

Organize your stuff by having a system for your shelves (see p. 32). Or cover and use old boxes (see p. 26 and p. 90). A papier-mâché bowl is useful for odds and ends (see p. 84), and a trellis makes a clever notice-board (see p. 35).

Chairs

Breathe new life into an old chair with a bright coat of paint, fake flowers, or animal stickers (see p. 54).

5 Comic COLOURS

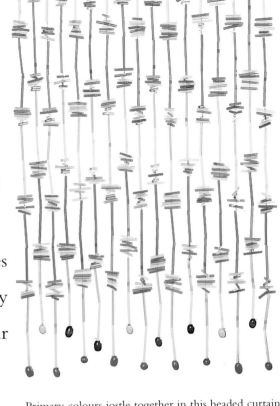

Brightly coloured cut-outs make great pictures when they're glued together in a **collage**. It's an easy way to **recycle** your old comics and to make your designs **completely original**.

Primary colours jostle together in this beaded curtain that brightens up any room (see p. 78).

Mix up portraits of your favourite stars to give hangers a new dimension (see p. 88).

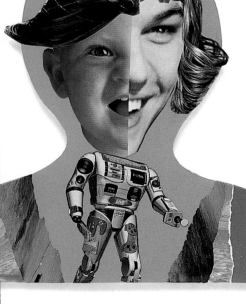

Computer magazines are full of vivid graphics that bring movement and energy to a frame (see p. 67).

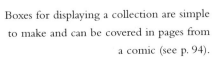

Boxes for displaying a collection are simple to make and can be covered in pages from a comic (see p. 94).

Shelves and screens

This room makes the most of recycled material. The shelves have a curtain of bubble wrap. It's pinned up behind a cardboard pelmet covered with comic scraps.

Frames

Make your own picture frames from scratch, using cardboard from old cereal boxes and more magazine cut-outs.

Cushions

Soft textures are important in making a room look comfortable, but you don't have to use traditional materials. Bubble wrap stuffed with discarded paper is one way of making a cushion (see p. 74).

Simple storage

Recycling can help solve storage problems, too. Re-cover boxes (see p. 90), or reinvent uses for plastic pockets (see p. 27) and kitchen gadgets (see p. 33).

Chairs

Turn your bedroom chair into a comic strip. Glue comic-strip cut-outs over a painted background.

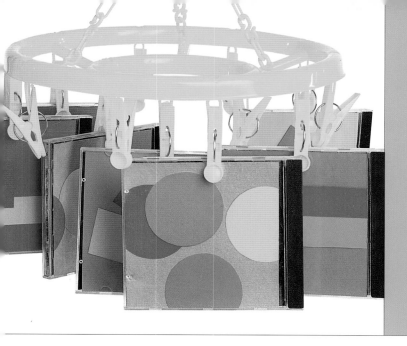

2 Sorting Your STUFF

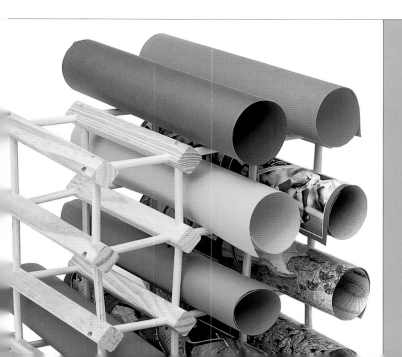

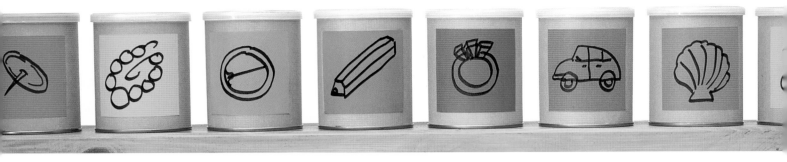

Contain
YOURSELF

Is your **stuff** taking over? Well, now's the time to get organized. Just by cleverly displaying your **collections** or clearing away clutter, you can create space and give your room a **cool look**. Gather together boxes and metal or plastic **containers** and give your things a home!

◄ **Tin boxes**
Odds and ends and keepsakes usually end up in messy piles or all mixed up together. Cheap plastic or metal stacking boxes keep everything separate.

◄ **Stacking systems**
Turn cardboard boxes into a storage system. Design your own labels to remind you what's in there – or write them in code to mystify intruders.

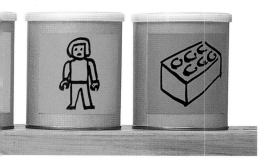

◄ Recycle it

Solve two problems at once by putting empty cartons to good use. Cover them with paper and a fun label, and use them to store anything from pennies to pins.

Pocket it ►

Plastic pockets are great for keeping clutter off your desk or the floor. Use them for odds and ends or to display your favourite things.

Bags of room ►

Plastic bags can be hung on pins with bulldog clips. They're good for stationery, or art supplies, and they let colour show through, too.

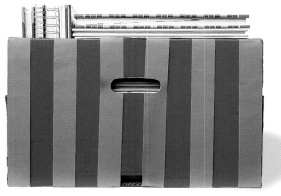

◄ Boxed in

Keep bulky things in boxes that you can put on a shelf or push under the bed. Keep books or sporting gear accessible, and pack away outgrown toys.

Ready to WEAR

Now put your clothes in order! Once you can see **what to wear at a glance** and once you have a place for everything from **underwear** to **sporting gear**, your room will instantly feel **user-friendly.** Make the items you wear most often **accessible** and pack away out-of-season clothes. **Give away** anything you've outgrown and put anything you're not using right **out of sight.** Sort your socks from your **pants** and give **shoes** a separate spot.

◄ Clothes ladder

A simple rope ladder makes an easy-to-reach clothes hanger for the items you wear most. Great for hanging up clothes at the end of the day, the ladder can also become a focal point of rainbow colours in your room.

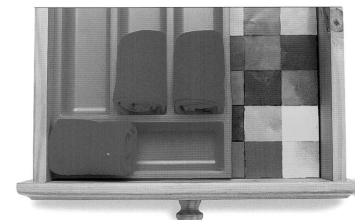

◄ Drawer clean up

Drawers quickly degenerate into a mess, especially when they are full of socks or pants. Make your own card dividers, or use a cutlery holder so that you can keep socks in pairs and sort them by colour.

Packing boxes ▶

Plastic containers add colour to your wardrobe and are useful for storing accessories, sports equipment, or less-used clothes, such as heavy sweaters in summer or T-shirts in winter.

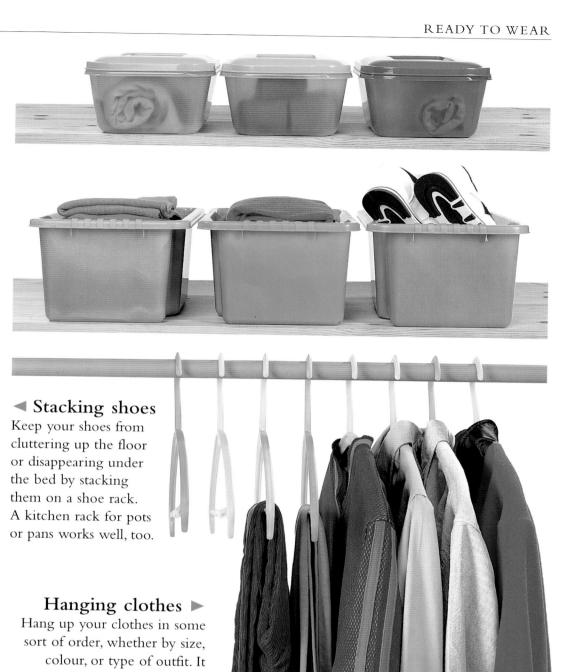

◀ Stacking shoes

Keep your shoes from cluttering up the floor or disappearing under the bed by stacking them on a shoe rack. A kitchen rack for pots or pans works well, too.

Hanging clothes ▶

Hang up your clothes in some sort of order, whether by size, colour, or type of outfit. It helps you see at a glance what you can wear each day and it creates more space.

For the wash ▶

Don't expect anyone else to know which clothes need washing in your room. A cheap plastic bucket is a simple – and fun – solution.

A Clear VIEW

Jam-packed jars are a great idea for little bits and pieces, or even for bugs. You'll easily see what's inside, and they look good side by side on a shelf.

Swift STORAGE

Keeping your space organized doesn't have to be boring. If you need **instant access** to your **favourite stuff** then it's time to take a stand. For an on-the-spot **clean up**, try using everyday objects where you least expect them. Keep the book you're reading close, and put CDs in their place with these **quick** and **clever props**.

A container of sand and some polished stones make cool pencil-holding bookends.

Colourful iron doorstops are often cheaper and more effective than purpose-made wooden bookends.

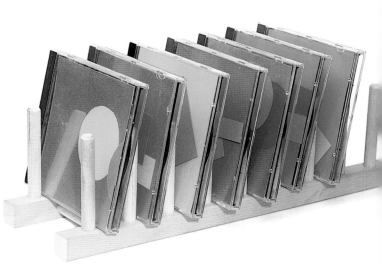

A wooden plate rack is a useful CD holder and it's less awkward than the plastic racks sold in stores.

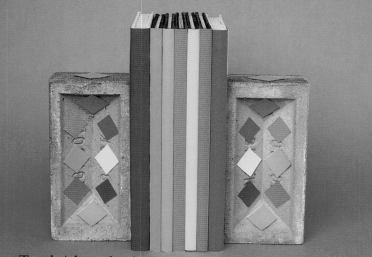

Two bricks make the simplest of bookends. Jazz them up a bit with coloured stickers or paper squares.

Household gadgets found in hardware stores can be adapted to tidy away your favourite CDs.

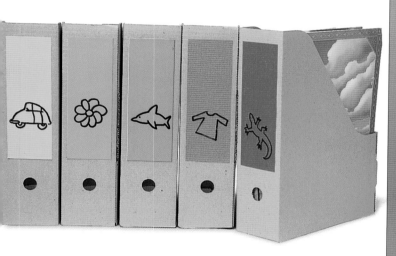

Simple cardboard magazine holders are good for tall books. Customize the labels yourself.

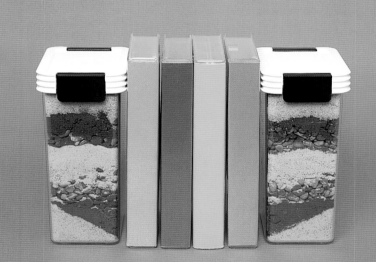

Look no further than the ground outside to create solid containers of earth, sand, and stones.

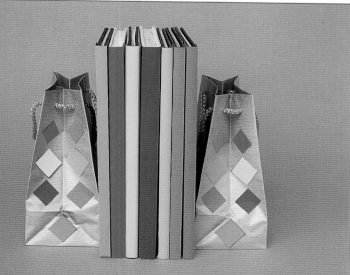

Small carrier bags filled with earth or pebbles make cheap and effective bookends.

Metal racks come in various shapes and sizes. Try them out for holding your CDs.

Paper CHASE

Lots of posters, postcards, homework, and drawings mean that your bedroom may contain more paper than a small office. You won't have room to put it all on the wall, and piles of paper look messy, but if you really want to keep every postcard from your best friend or save all your football charts, then you need to choose an off-the-wall way to store them.

A line of cards ▲

A simple clothes-line and coloured pegs are a great way to show off your favourite postcards. You can change them easily and even hang up important notes. This is a good idea for birthday cards too!

Packing posters

Effective bottle storage also works for rolls of paper. A partitioned cardboard box is ideal for keeping rolled-up posters uncrushed. Equally good is a wooden wine rack. The posters look colourful and are then easy to swap with the ones already on your wall.

On file ▶

Keep all your personal or school notes in handy files. If there is loose paper to store, slip it into plastic folders that you can file away.

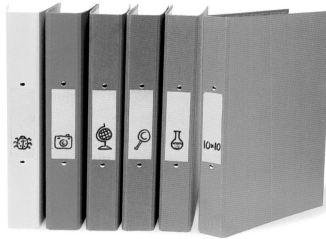

◀ Pin it up

A pinboard is an obvious way to store and display notes, tickets, letters, and loose paper. Keep it up to date by throwing away old notes or reminders.

Trellis ▶

Bring texture to your walls and originality to your papers by using pegs, clips, and a trellis to display any memento you like.

Showing
OFF

You may not think you're a "collector", but you probably have at least one group of **similar objects** scattered around your room. **Souvenirs** from holidays, **figurines** from the hamburger joint, favourite cars or **sports heroes** may be hidden among the clutter of boxes and old toys. **Now's the time** to get them out and show them off. A **queue of traffic**, a cluster of cats, or a group of snow shakers adds **colour**, **shape**, and even **comedy** to an otherwise ordinary set of shelves.

3 Decorating BASICS

Getting Started

★Adult help!

Always get permission before you start transforming the things in your room. You may need a hand assembling all the tools and materials, and you may need extra help on some of the projects.

★Pace yourself

Be sure to leave enough time for a project, taking into account drying times as well as the time you need for cleaning up and putting things back.

★Cover up

Cover up if you are painting, protect furniture and floors with newspapers, plastic, or an old sheet. If you are working on a table or desk, cover its surface before you begin. Always cut on top of a thick plastic mat. Cover yourself with old clothes such as a long-sleeved shirt, old trousers and shoes. You may need rubber gloves for dyeing or painting. Tie back long hair.

★Read instructions

Make sure you read and understand the

and...

instructions on the materials you are using as well as the pages you are following in this book.

★Get ready

Collect everything you need at the start. It's very annoying to begin a project and then have to stop everything while you go to find the glue – worse still if you have to go out to buy it!

★Practise first

If you're unsure, practise first. Use an old piece of wood, a spare piece of cloth or paper – whatever you need to get comfortable with the tools or to see the effect you're planning to create.

...Finishing Off

★Clean up well

Wash brushes, wipe away any spilled paint and glue, throw away any remnants, and wash your hands.

Emulsion paint

Emulsion paint is water-based so it's fairly easy to clean off your hands and wash off your brushes. For large areas of wall, use matt emulsion. For pieces of furniture, such as chairs or chests of drawers, use vinyl silk emulsion which produces a slight sheen and a wipe-clean surface. You can add water to emulsion to thin it a little too.

Painting and Varnishing

Acrylic paint

This water-based paint is useful for most craft jobs, such as decorating paper pots (see p. 84), painting over a base such as zebra stripes on a chair (see p. 57), or as an alternative to emulsion for various paint effects. It is more elastic than poster paints and can be used as is or thinned down with water.

Acrylic paint and PVA mix

A mixture of equal parts paint and PVA glue (see p. 45) helps toughen the paint. The paint then applies better to smooth surfaces. This mix also produces a finish with a slight sheen. It is useful for transforming boxes (see p. 90).

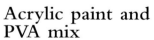

The materials shown here are used to make the projects featured in this book. They are all available in craft shops and hardware stores. Remember to ask for adult help when using them.

Spray paint

For small, rough areas where you want to get an even coat of paint into awkward corners (see the gold picture frame on p. 66), you can use spray paint. Be careful, though – these sprays give off fumes. You should spray outside and cover up the area around the object you are spraying.

Brushes

You need to use a size of brush that fits the job you are doing. The larger the brush, the bigger the area you will cover at one time. However, the smaller the brush, the more delicate you can be. For all the projects in this book, brush sizes range from fine artist's brushes, to decorating brushes 4 cm wide. These 4 cm brushes are good for painting chairs and chests (see p. 54 and p. 58). If you are painting an area of wall as a base for a paint effect (see p. 50), you will need a brush that's about 6 cm wide.

Fabric paints and dyes

These silk dyes are painted directly onto fabric. They are water-based and very runny so you can achieve a smudged or blended effect if colours overlap (see p. 68). To fix the paint to the fabric you need to run a hot iron over it. For dyeing fabric (see p. 70), you can use cold water dye – but make sure you follow the makers' instructions. Use pure cotton or other non-synthetic fabrics for the brightest finished result.

Varnish

Varnish will not only make your project look brighter, it will also protect it from scuffs and scratches. There are many types, but the one used for projects here (such as decorating doorknobs on p. 62 and papier mâché pots on p. 84), is a water-based acrylic varnish. It can be painted onto most things and will need two or three coats. At first, it produces a blue tinge, but this disappears as it dries.

Cutting and Sticking

Getting stuck in is half the fun of creating your own designs, but it's helpful to know which glues are which before you start. Think about how you will cut things out, too, and let an adult know if you are going to use a craft knife. All the materials you need are readily available in DIY centres and art shops.

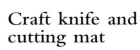

Craft knife and cutting mat

A craft knife has a very sharp, angled blade that is usually retractable. Use a ruler to help you cut straight, clean lines through cardboard. Always place a rubber cutting mat underneath so that you don't cut into a work surface.

Scissors

For all thicknesses and weights of paper, except thick cardboard (see above), use scissors for cutting out shapes or strips. Strong kitchen scissors are ideal, but if you have small hands, use a smaller pair with finer blades. Small scissors are more useful for elaborate shapes as well.

PVA glue

PVA stands for "polyvinyl acetate" and is white glue that dries clear. It's useful for gluing paper and can be mixed with acrylic paint for a strong, shiny finish.

Craft glue

This is a clear, strong glue that you squeeze from a tube. It spreads easily over most surfaces and is useful for anything from fabrics to frames.

Glue stick

Mess-free and convenient, this glue is ideal for sticking paper together. Spread it as evenly as you can – it sometimes comes off the stick in small lumps.

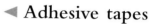

◀ Adhesive tapes

You can buy a variety of sticky tapes for a variety of uses. The clear type is fairly permanent, while white, opaque tape is useful for temporarily holding something in place. White tape is easily removed without leaving a mark.

Needles and thread ▶

Use a medium-size needle and cotton thread for sewing fabric (see p. 74). For threading beads or straws (see p. 78) use a darning needle.

◀ Wallpaper paste

This is ideal for papier mâché since it sticks newspaper together and hardens as it dries.

Filler ▶

Ready-mixed all-purpose filler, used for fixing small holes in walls or woodwork, makes a good base for attaching decorations such as beads or buttons (see p. 62). You can paint it after it sets.

Beads, Nuts, Bolts, Sweet Wrappers, Coloured Foil,

Things to Collect

Take a look around you to discover all kinds of bits and pieces that are perfect for your decorating projects. There's even inspiration in things that usually go in the rubbish. You don't need to spend lots of money on trimmings, just start collecting!

Shells, Pebbles, Magazines, Comics, Cartons, Boxes,

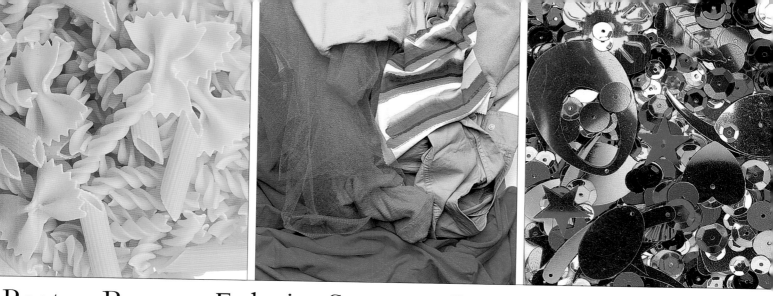

Pasta, Beans, Fabric Scraps, Sequins, Ribbons,

Jewels, Straws, Crisp Packets, Buttons, Plastic Toys

4 Making CHANGES

Paint EFFECTS

W ake up your walls – or your wardrobe doors – with fabulous paint patterns. Follow the easy techniques shown on these pages and let your imagination run wild! Choose bold, bright colours and design your own patterns. Then decorate part or all of your walls for a style that's unique.

4

5

6

7

Paint Effects

First choose your paint – either acrylic or emulsion is best for the designs on this page. Gather together odds and ends such as sponges, plastic bags, bubble wrap, cling film, corks, string, and cardboard tubes. Or make your own simple cut-outs. Try these out on scrap paper first to decide what shapes and colours you want to use. Then start on a small area of wall. Make sure you are happy with the result before you cover a larger area.

Paint effects 1 and 2

Draw your design on a kitchen sponge and cut out the shape. Cut out a square of corrugated cardboard. Glue the cut-out sponge shape to the piece of cardboard. Stick another smaller piece of card to the back to make a handle. Pour a shallow layer of paint onto a plate and lightly dip the sponge in it. Gently press the sponge on the wall. Use even pressure and lift the sponge straight off for a smudge-free edge. For a lined effect, simply dip a piece of corrugated cardboard into the paint and press it on your wall.

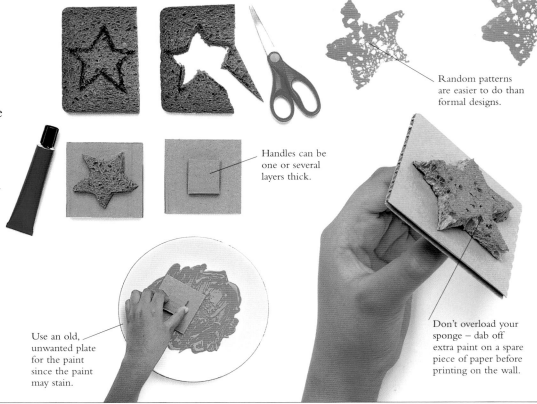

Random patterns are easier to do than formal designs.

Handles can be one or several layers thick.

Use an old, unwanted plate for the paint since the paint may stain.

Don't overload your sponge – dab off extra paint on a spare piece of paper before printing on the wall.

Paint effects 3 and 6

You can make an irregular pattern on your wall by scrunching up a plastic bag. Pour a shallow layer of paint onto an old plate – if the paint is too deep the finished pattern will be blotchy. Dip the bag in the paint. You will probably get around three prints for each time you dip. For a tighter pattern try using an open-textured sponge. Dip it in the paint, then dab it on your wall. Repeat until the area is covered.

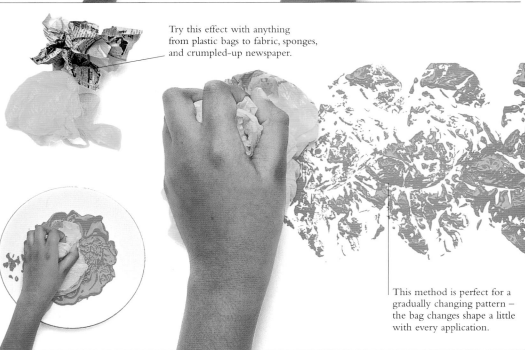

Try this effect with anything from plastic bags to fabric, sponges, and crumpled-up newspaper.

This method is perfect for a gradually changing pattern – the bag changes shape a little with every application.

Paint effect 4

Draw a design on a piece of stiff paper – solid, simple shapes are easiest to use. Cut out your design. Next pour paint onto an old plate. Dip a sponge in the paint. Hold the stencil firmly in place on the wall with one hand. Dab the paint-filled sponge over it and then carefully lift the stencil off the wall.

Sponge well into the corners of the stencil, but don't let the paint run underneath it.

Paint effect 5

Stick masking tape to your wall for strong geometric patterns and clean, straight lines. Dip a sponge in paint and dab it firmly over the whole area. When the paint is dry, carefully remove the tape. The taped area will stay the colour of your original wall. The rest of the area will pick up the paint in stripes or checks.

The tape masks out the covered area, leaving it the original background colour.

Use a thin layer of paint to cover the wall.

Paint effect 7

For a dotted design try using bubble wrap. Cut out a manageable shape – a small square or oblong piece should be fine. Next pour a shallow layer of paint onto an old plate. Dip the bubble wrap in the paint, then press it gently onto your wall. Peel off the bubble wrap and repeat.

If your bubble wrap gets clogged with paint, rinse it under the tap or use another piece.

It can take about 20 minutes for the paint to dry.

Changing CHAIRS

Bring a chair to life by painting it with zebra stripes or sticking on paper butterflies and fake flowers. Give it a kick by covering it with team colours and a football photo. If you want to keep your chair under wraps instead of under piles of clothes, try covering it in kitchen foil, or spice it up with fake fur or a fantastic feather boa.

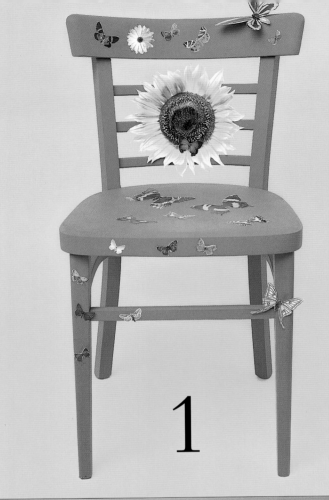

1

3

2

4

5

Changing Chairs

You'll need to use an old chair that no one minds you decorating. If you are not allowed to paint a chair, choose a method that just covers it up. The chair to be painted needs to be clean, so wash it with soap and water. Then collect the other things that you will need – sandpaper, a paintbrush, paint, magazine pictures, kitchen foil, fake fur, or whatever you want to use.

Wrap the sandpaper around a wooden block for extra grip.

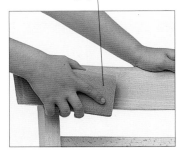

a) If your chair is rough, rub it with sandpaper – medium-weight sandpaper works well on most wood.

Use vinyl silk emulsion paint for a bright, long-lasting finish, and choose a brush that's about 4 cm wide.

b) You will need to give your chair a base coat first. Paint this on roughly and then leave it to dry.

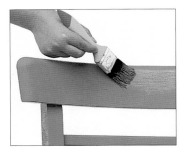

c) Your second coat is the one that shows, so keep your strokes even and don't overload your brush.

Decorating chair 1

It's fun to decorate your chair using cut-outs such as flowers, butterflies, cars, or stars. You can use pictures from old magazines, posters, or your sticker collection. Cut out the shapes and then stick them on your painted chair with PVA glue. Brush them with varnish.

If any glue spills out, quickly wipe it off with a clean cloth.

Varnish the cut-out pictures to protect them and make them sparkle.

Decorating chair 2

Paint the chair in one of your team's colours. Then cut out strips of paper in the team's other colours. Make sure you have the right lengths to wrap around the chair. Brush the strips with PVA glue and stick them carefully onto the chair, one colour at a time. Smooth them in place.

A bold pictur makes a goo focal poin

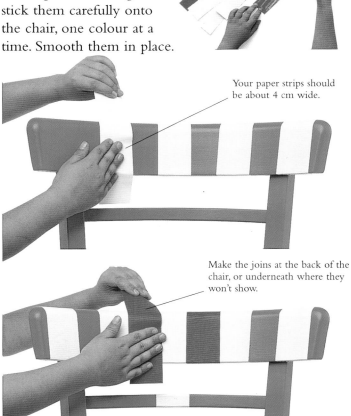

Your paper strips should be about 4 cm wide.

Make the joins at the back of the chair, or underneath where they won't show.

Decorating chair 3

Animals have amazing markings and you can copy or adapt them. Use a picture for reference – choose one that clearly shows the animal's pattern. Paint your chair in one of the animal's basic colours. Draw on the markings in pencil and fill them in with acrylic paint.

Decorating chair 4

Cook up an instant transformation by covering your chair with kitchen foil. Tear off pieces of foil and scrunch them into position. Secure any stray ends with clear tape. Instead of kitchen foil, you can use this method with fabric, brown wrapping paper, or colourful gift wrap.

Use clear tape to hold the kitchen foil in place.

Scrunch the foil tightly round the chair to completely cover it.

Animals with strong, clear markings are easiest to copy.

Make sure the base coat is dry before your draw on your design.

Use a fine paintbrush to keep the design neat.

Decorating chair 5

Give your chair a new look and feel by adding an interesting texture. Feathery fake fur looks exotic, especially when it's an electric colour. Simply tape down one end, wrap the fur around the chair and secure.

Long pieces of fake fur are easier to work with than short pieces.

Experiment with designs before you stick the fur into place.

Chest of DRAWERS

Turn your drawers into a chest you can treasure by painting it with **patterns** or covering it with **cut-outs**. Whether you choose a freehand design of **whirls** and **swirls** or a **two-tone** cow print, paint is a simple option. Or you can add some action with a **collage** of comic strips. For something more ornate, create a **gold-sprayed relief** of pasta and string.

1

2

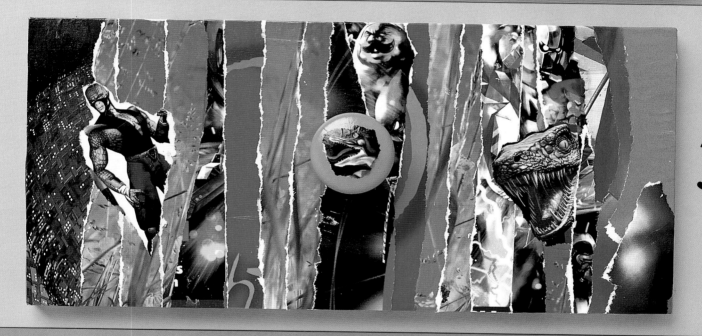

3

4

Chest of Drawers

Preparing the sides and back of the chest

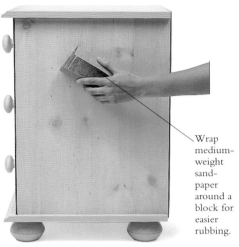

Wrap medium-weight sand-paper around a block for easier rubbing.

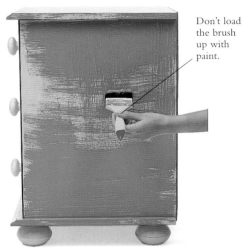

Don't load the brush up with paint.

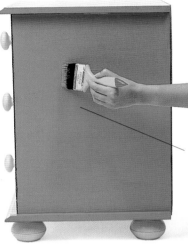

Each coat of paint should be kept thin so that you get a smooth finish.

a) First gather together the materials you will need. Then prepare the surface by smoothing down any old paint or rough wood with sandpaper.

b) Using vinyl silk emulsion paint for a shiny finish, apply the first coat. Move the paintbrush up and down, then side to side.

c) When the first coat is dry, apply the second coat, working the brush as you did for the first coat. This will give you an even finish.

Decorating chest 1

Sand down the front surface of the chest. Mark your design on the chest using a pencil. For stronger lines, use a permanent marker. Apply the first colour of paint and let it dry before you paint on the second. This design uses interacting shapes that you can paint in contrasting colours.

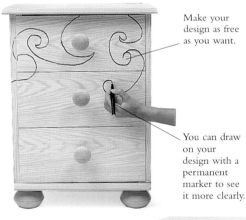

Make your design as free as you want.

You can draw on your design with a permanent marker to see it more clearly.

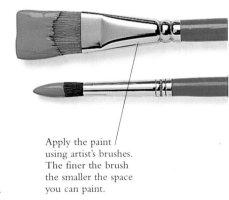

Apply the paint using artist's brushes. The finer the brush the smaller the space you can paint.

Use the fine brush for tight corners.

Include the drawer knobs in your colour scheme.

Decorating chest 2

Paint the chest of drawers with two coats of white vinyl silk emulsion paint. When it is dry, pencil in your design on the chest. Use a fine artist's brush to paint in the blobs with black acrylic paint.

Keep your design bold and allow some of the blobs to go off the edge.

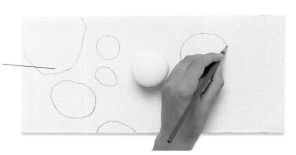

Include the drawer knob in your design.

Decorating chest 3

Paint the back and sides of the chest of drawers, but leave the front uncovered. Tear strips out of the pages of magazines or comics and glue these onto the chest. Take cut-outs from the same magazines and stick these on top of the strips. Brush two coats of varnish over the whole design.

Choose strips and pictures from a similar colour range and glue them on with a glue stick.

Make the strips long enough to fold over the top and bottom of the drawer.

Choose a special picture for the handle.

Paint with varnish to protect the paper.

Decorating chest 4

For this ornate, formal design, you'll need to take the chest of drawers outside, place it on newspaper, and spray paint the back and sides with gold paint. For the drawers, use craft glue to attach pasta and string to the drawer fronts. Then spray these with gold paint too.

First, spread the glue where you are going to make your design.

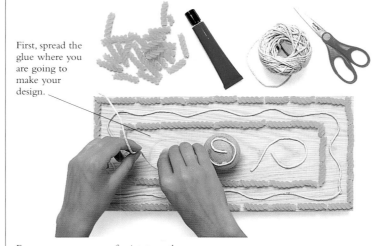

For an even coverage of paint, turn the drawer around and spray it a second time.

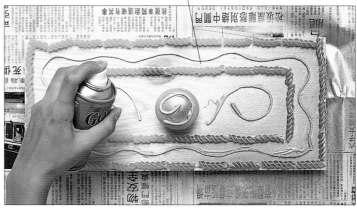

Decorating
HANDLES

Make your mark on the door to your room by decorating your doorknob. You can hint at a **theme** inside your room – seascapes, polka dots, or glitzy glamour – or discourage visitors from bugging you. Mix and match **colours** and **textures** so your handles look and feel great! Then try out your **ideas** on wardrobe and chest-of-drawer handles, too.

Use ready-mixed, all-purpose filler.

a) Spread filler straight onto the handle. Spread newspaper underneath to catch any blobs.

Plan your design before adding the beads.

b) Gently press decorations into the filler. Leave the handle to dry for about 30 minutes.

Acrylic paint is the best type to use.

c) When the filler is dry, use a fine artist's brush to cover it with gold paint.

For the seashore look, press shells into the filler. To finish, brush on a water-based varnish.

Paint your handles with a bright acrylic paint, and then glue on anything you like!

Stick bits of coloured foil and sweet wrappers onto the handle for a bright, theatrical effect.

Get down to the nuts and bolts by sticking them on with craft glue and painting with varnish.

Choose a small handful of multicoloured beads for a perfect Aladdin appearance.

A is for "anything goes" when it comes to giving a personal touch to your room.

Buttons give instant colour. Glue them onto a plain handle, and coat with varnish.

Go dotty with simple stickers. Brush them with varnish to help keep the spots in place.

Keep out! Varnished bugs, beasts, or aliens give unwanted guests the creeps.

PICTURE Frames

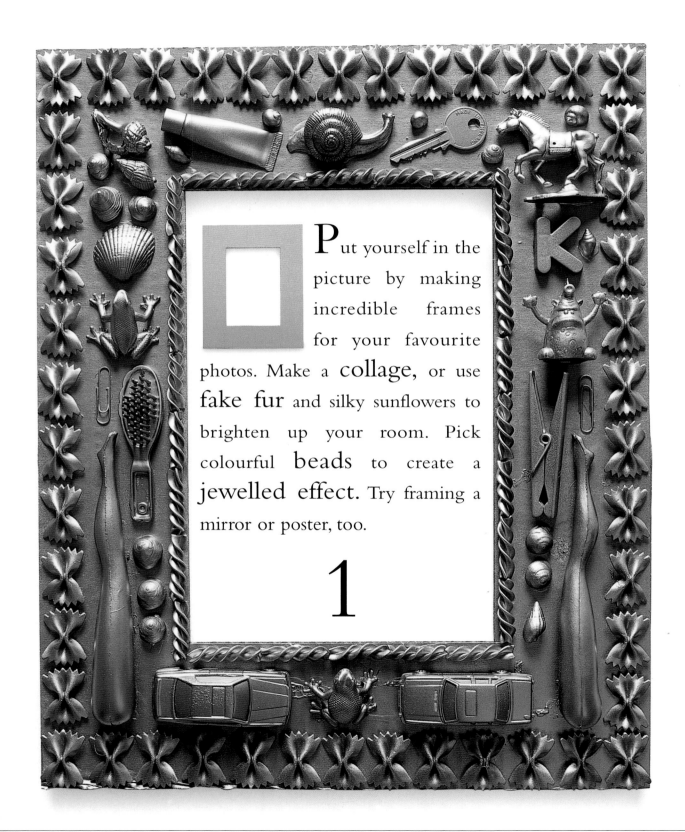

Put yourself in the picture by making incredible frames for your favourite photos. Make a collage, or use fake fur and silky sunflowers to brighten up your room. Pick colourful beads to create a jewelled effect. Try framing a mirror or poster, too.

1

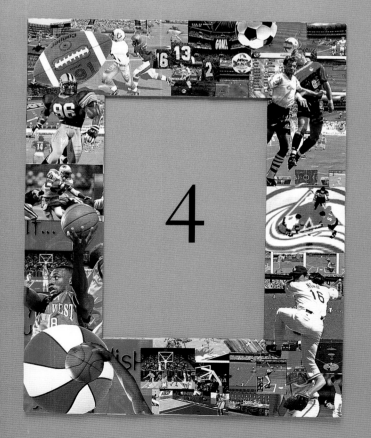

Picture Frames

Making the basic frame

The frame will hang best if you stick the string to the top part of it.

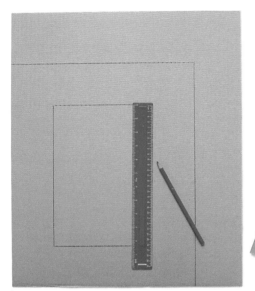

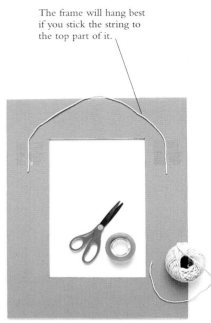

a) Measure out a frame on a large sheet of cardboard. Make it wide enough – about 8 cm – to create a design.

b) Cut out the frame using a ruler and craft knife. Keep the middle window smaller than the picture to be framed.

c) Tape string to the back, or if the frame will be heavy, knot string through holes in the card.

You can use any object that will stick.

Things that are the same shape make a good border.

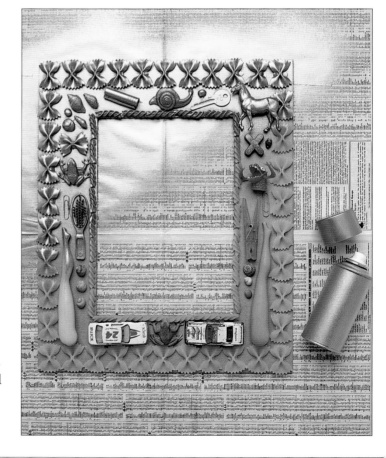

Making frame 1

Collect together small objects such as pasta bows and old toys. Lay them out on the frame – a roughly symmetrical pattern works best. Once you are happy with the result, stick the pieces down with craft glue. Lay the frame on newspaper, and spray with gold paint.

Making frame 2

Spread craft glue on the cardboard. Stick the cardboard to the fake fur. Trim the corners of the fur. Cut an X in the fabric inside the frame; then trim the fabric and glue it in place. Attach string and decorate.

The glue shouldn't be too thick

Making frame 5

Cut out small squares of cardboard that are as wide as your frame. Use craft glue to stick them neatly around the frame. Next paint the frame with gold acrylic paint. When the paint is dry, glue on shiny beads and bright buttons.

Building up layers of card will make a simple frame more interesting.

Choose light fabric flowers to stick to the front of your frame.

Making frames 3 and 4

Cut out your basic frame; then choose colourful magazine pages and tear or cut them into strips. Cut out pictures of sports heroes, cartoon characters, or other images. Lay the strips over the frame and glue them in position, wrapping the ends around the back. Stick the cut-out characters over these to create an action-packed collage. You could try the same thing with pictures of stars from favourite movies and bands.

Paint or DYE

Transform white cotton fabric by using paint or dye. Make rainbow stripes, spiral shapes, or bright checks. And for circles and swirls, knot up your material for tie-dye. Once you create your unique designs, sew different pieces together to make anything from cushion covers to bedspreads.

5

6

Paint or Dye

Painting fabric

Start off by choosing a piece of fabric – 100% cotton is best because it is cheap and it takes dye well. Paint on your designs using silk dyes. These are very runny and blend together for some unexpected results. Painting fabric can be messy, so protect your work surface by covering it with several layers of newspaper. Cut your fabric into a manageable size; then lay it flat on the newspaper. Use tape to secure it in place. Choose a medium-sized paintbrush and make sure it is perfectly clean before you dip it in the silk dye.

Paint or dye 1

Paint a spiral pattern from the middle outwards, one colour at a time. Let the colours run together for a well-blended look.

Paint or dye 2, 3, and 4

Paint the stripes from top to bottom for a clear view of your work.

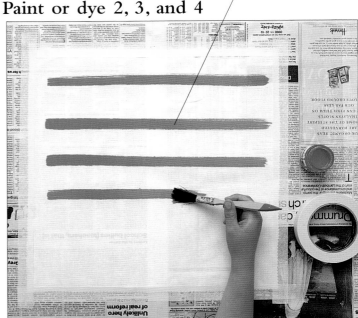

a) Load up your brush; then paint coloured lines onto the fabric. Try to space the lines at regular intervals.

Dyeing fabric

This tie-dyeing pattern is made using a cold-water dye. The steps shown here are a general guide, but make sure you follow the method described on the dye packet. Use cotton fabric since this absorbs the dye best. And always wear rubber gloves when you handle the wet cotton, since the dye will stain your skin.

Paint or dye 5 and 6

Any area of the fabric bound by rubber bands or string will not absorb the dye and will remain white. One method of tie-dyeing is to tie buttons into the fabric. This leaves you with a pattern of small circles.

a) Puncture the container of dye and sprinkle the powder into a litre of water. Let the dye dissolve.

b) Add the bag of fixative and the required quantity of salt. Stir the mixture until everything is dissolved.

Choose bright
strong colours for a
dramatic effect.

Leave some fabric
unpainted for bright,
white markings.

Make sure you don't
rest your wrist on the
wet paint.

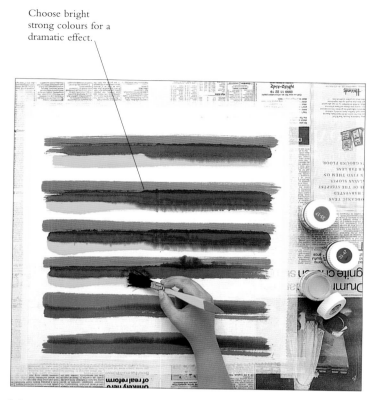

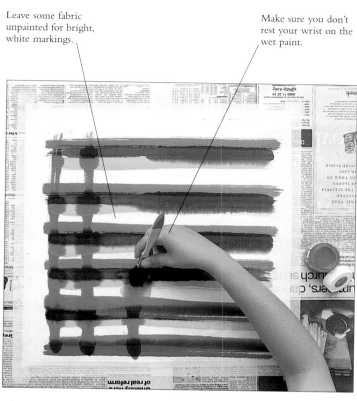

b) Before each set of lines is dry, begin the next colour. It doesn't matter if your lines are not perfectly straight.

c) Paint vertical stripes or dots in the spaces. Or try painting more horizontal stripes. Iron the fabric to set the dyes.

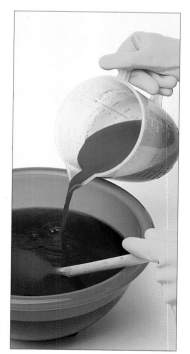

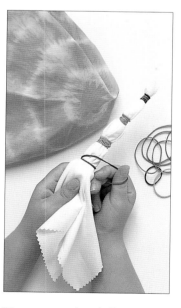

c) Pour the dye mixture into a bowl of warm water. Stir the contents of the bowl until thoroughly mixed.

d) Immerse your tied-up fabric in the dye. Make sure it is completely soaked. Then leave it for one hour.

e) Squeeze out the fabric and rinse away the excess dye. Let the fabric dry and then remove the buttons.

You can make different tie-dye designs by changing the way you tie the rubber bands. For a hoop design, fold fabric from the middle and tie rubber bands at intervals.

Customize CUSHIONS

Whether you go for junk-filled bubble wrap or brilliant bows, colourful cacti or sparkling tinsel, rainbow stripes or zebra patterns, you can re-invent the cushion for your bedroom. Bright colours and cool designs will work wonders – they'll add life to an old chair, a dull corner, or a tired bed.

1

Customize Cushions

Making a cushion cover

You can customize a ready-made cushion cover, but if you want to make one of your own, here's how. Start by cutting out two pieces of fabric that are about 35 cm x 35 cm, or the size that will fit an existing cushion. Pin these together. Starting about 1.5 cm from the edge, sew the two pieces together. Leave a 25 cm space on one edge to allow room for the cushion. Trim off the corners, then turn the case inside out. Push in a cushion pad and neatly sew up the open edge.

Pin the fabric together with the right sides facing each other.

Cushion 1

Cushion covers don't need to be made from fabric, so why not experiment? Bubble wrap, for example, makes an unusual cushion. Cut out a long oblong piece – 30 cm x 60 cm is about the right size for a small cushion. Tape two of the open sides together, and then fill the cushion with empty crisp packets, sweet papers, fabric, or any other soft, colourful item you have around. Once the cushion is full, tape it up.

The piece of bubble wrap should be twice the width of the cushion you want to make.

Bring the sides to meet in the middle.

Use clear tape to stick the edges together.

Don't overfill the bag or the seams will split.

Fold over the open edges, and then seal with tape.

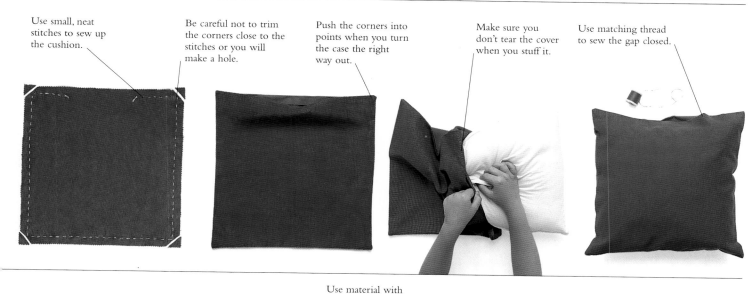

Use small, neat stitches to sew up the cushion.

Be careful not to trim the corners close to the stitches or you will make a hole.

Push the corners into points when you turn the case the right way out.

Make sure you don't tear the cover when you stuff it.

Use matching thread to sew the gap closed.

Wrap the ribbon around the cushion as you would decorate a present.

Use material with interesting textures.

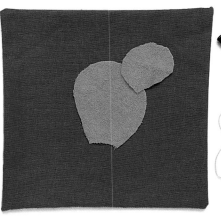

Cushions 2 and 4

Use the fabric you designed using paint or dye to make colourful cushion covers. For an even brighter variation, add a ribbon, tied in a simple bow.

Cushion 3

Cut out shapes from scrap material and glue them onto the fabric. Use bold stitches to help hold the fabric in place – they can become part of the design, too..

Curl the tinsel into balls before sewing it on the cushion.

Stick the stripes on with craft glue.

Cushion 5

Sew a piece of tinsel around the edge of the cushion, and then sew more tinsel onto the front and back. Try using ribbons, buttons, or pieces of fun fur.

Cushion 6

Create a dramatic animal pattern, such as these zebra stripes. Simply cut out strips from a piece of felt and glue them straight onto the cushion cover.

Big SCREENS

B eads, bugs, buttons, as well as hundreds of colourful straws – these are some of the ingredients you can use for a brilliant range of blinds or screens. Hang them over your window, a bookcase, or set of shelves.

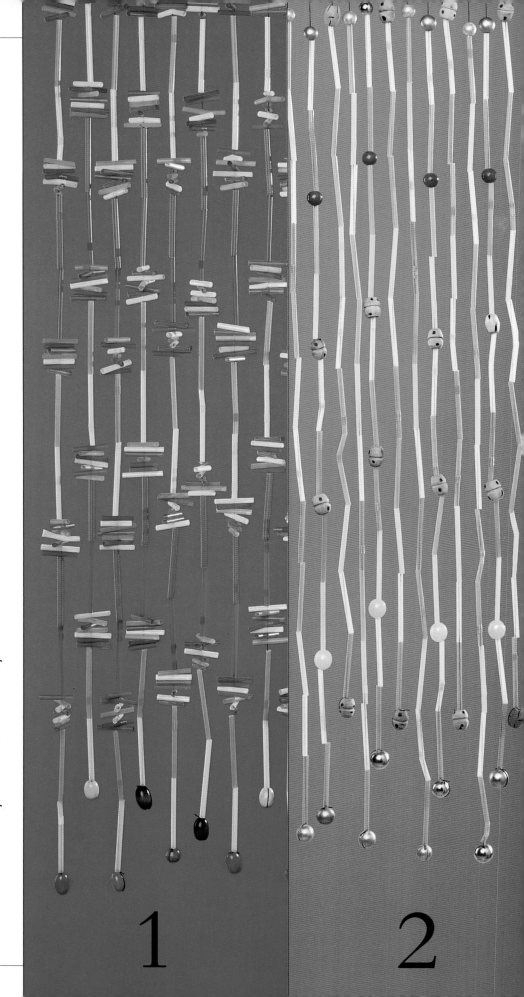

1

2

3

4

Making Screens

First you will need to measure the height and width of the area to be covered by your screen. It's a good idea to measure twice to make sure you get the right measurement. Then allow about 3 cm extra all round. Choose a dowel or bamboo pole that is wider than the screen you want to make. Paint it with an acrylic paint that complements the colours you choose for the screen. Leave the pole until it is completely dry.

You'll need to screw hooks into a window frame to hold the blind.

Gather together all your materials before you start the blind.

Making screen 1

Measure out a long piece of strong thread. Thread the needle; then pass it through a wooden bead. Tie the bead in place with a secure knot. Cut the straws into different lengths, and pass the needle through two longer ones. Make a bundle of six or seven short lengths, lay them horizontally, and pierce them with the needle. Continue the pattern, leaving enough thread to attach the line to the pole. When finished, hang the screen on the hooks.

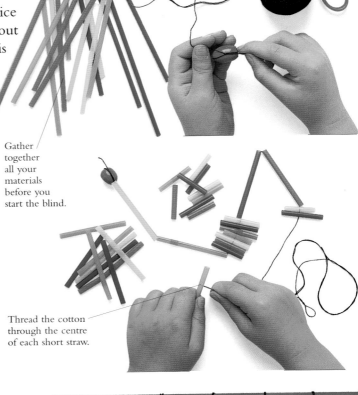

Thread the cotton through the centre of each short straw.

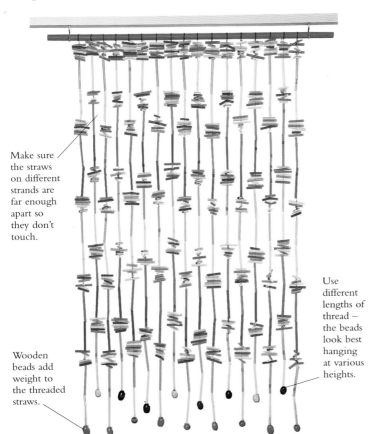

Make sure the straws on different strands are far enough apart so they don't touch.

Wooden beads add weight to the threaded straws.

Use different lengths of thread – the beads look best hanging at various heights.

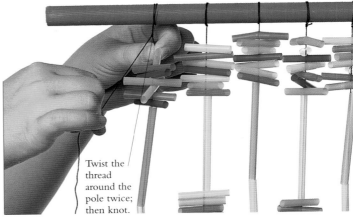

Twist the thread around the pole twice; then knot.

Make sure the pole is evenly balanced on the hooks.

Making screen 2

Secure a bead on the end of your thread. Then alternate coloured straws and add another bead. Continue in this way until the thread is covered. Other strands can have coloured straws and just a couple of beads.

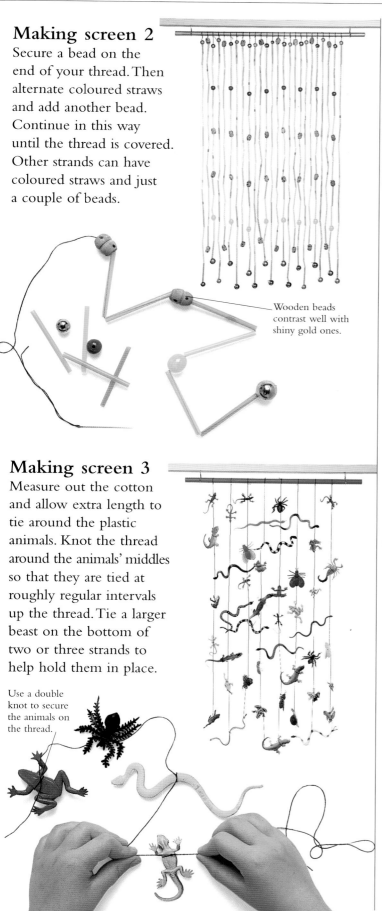

Wooden beads contrast well with shiny gold ones.

Making screen 3

Measure out the cotton and allow extra length to tie around the plastic animals. Knot the thread around the animals' middles so that they are tied at roughly regular intervals up the thread. Tie a larger beast on the bottom of two or three strands to help hold them in place.

Use a double knot to secure the animals on the thread.

Making screen 4

Cut out a piece of transparent material such as muslin, bubble wrap, or bold-coloured tulle. Allow about 4 cm of extra length at the top to wrap around the pole. Lay your material out flat and smooth out any wrinkles; then attach it to the pole using blobs of PVA glue. Use colourful sweet wrappers, buttons, and bits of foil to decorate the rest of the screen.

Make your basic blind before you begin to decorate.

Attach foil shapes to hide any blobs of glue.

Lay out your design before you stick it all in place.

The sweet-wrapping edging gives the blind colourful symmetry.

When it hangs against the light the material appears see-through.

Bright
IDEAS

The some new light on your room by transforming any plain lampshade. You can stick on anything from spots to snakes, paint it with stripes or swirls, cover it with a cut-out skirt, or sew on glimmering jewels. It will look fun, and the atmosphere of the whole room will change for the better.

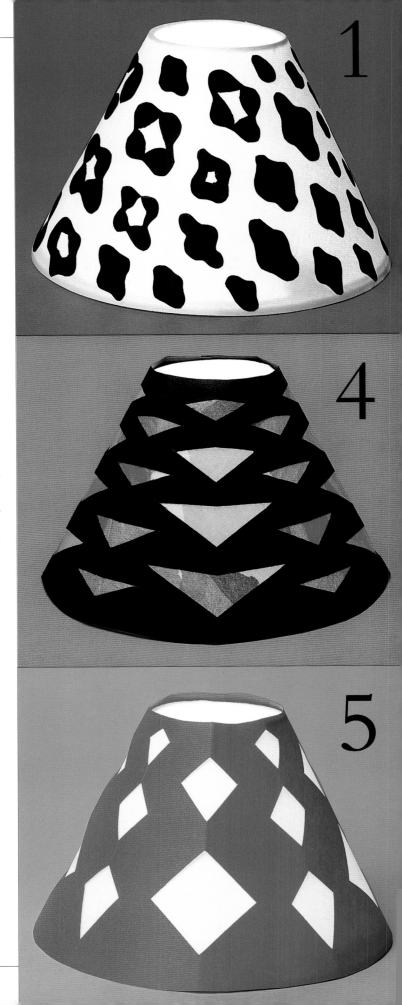

1

4

5

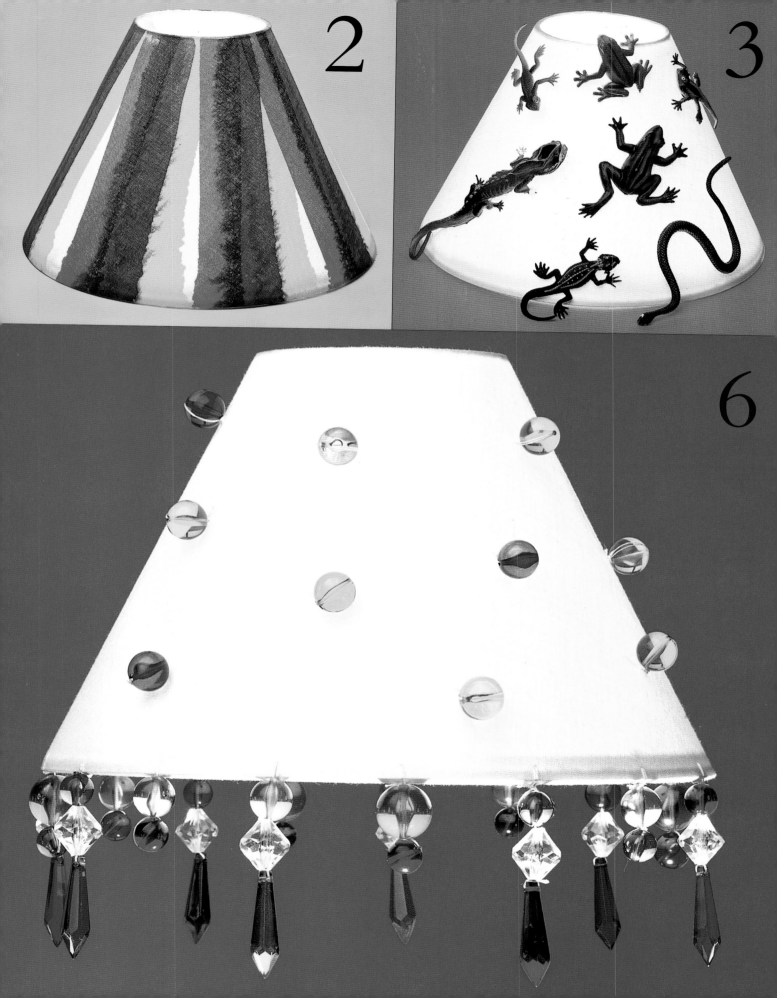

2

3

6

Bright Ideas

First, unplug the lamp and detach the shade before you start. If it's a hanging shade, you may need help getting it down. Whatever design you choose, always leave the top uncovered to allow the bulb's heat to escape. Depending on the look you want, you will need to find some card, silk dyes, fabric paints, felt pens, glue, a paintbrush, or some beads.

Glue the shapes on with a glue stick.

Decorating lamp 1
For animal prints, like this cheetah pattern, look for a photograph that you can copy, and then draw the shapes onto black card. Cut these out and simply glue them onto a plain white or cream shade.

Decorating lamp 5
You can make your own paper shade to slip over an existing one so that the light shines though a pattern of cut-outs. Roll the shade over a sheet of paper, drawing its outline. Cut out the shade shape and fold it in half. Fold it again. Leave a space at the top for gluing, and cut shapes out of the two folded edges. Glue the outer edges together and slip the cover over your original shade.

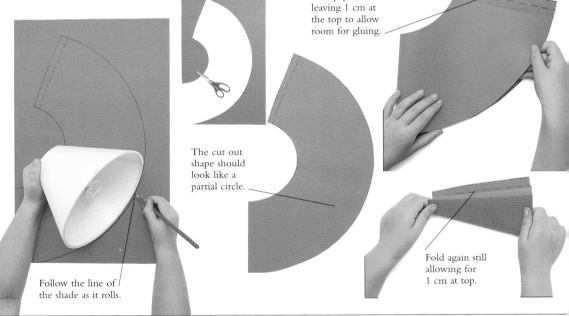

Follow the line of the shade as it rolls.

The cut out shape should look like a partial circle.

Fold paper, leaving 1 cm at the top to allow room for gluing.

Fold again still allowing for 1 cm at top.

Decorating lamp 6
For this lamp, sew single glass beads directly onto the fabric of your shade. To attach the beads around the rim, thread several together as shown and then pass the needle through the beads again before sewing them onto the rim of the shade. Try alternating long beads and round ones for the edge.

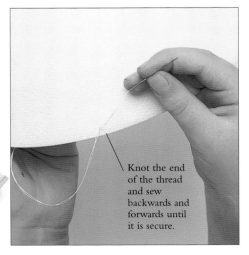

Knot the end of the thread and sew backwards and forwards until it is secure.

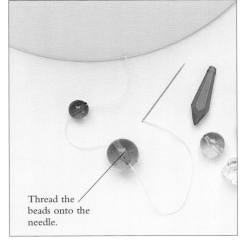

Thread the beads onto the needle.

Decorating lamp 2

Painting the shade with silk dyes or fabric paints is one of the easiest ways to transform your lamp. You can practise a design on some old fabric beforehand. If you don't have dyes or paint, try using thick felt pens.

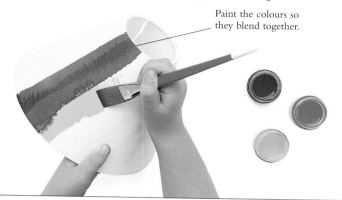

Paint the colours so they blend together.

Decorating lamp 3

For a dramatic or creepy effect, glue bugs, beasts, or bats to your lampshade. Toy shops usually sell cheap collections of plastic animals that you can stick on with craft glue.

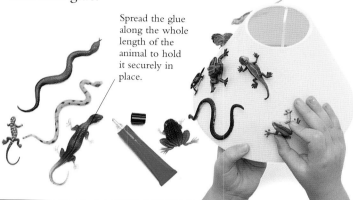

Spread the glue along the whole length of the animal to hold it securely in place.

Don't cut shapes out of the edges left for gluing

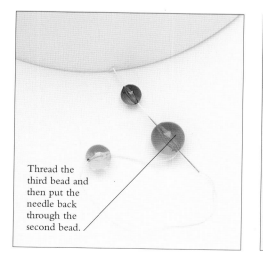

Lamp 4

For an illuminated stained-glass effect, glue coloured tissue paper or cellophane to the back of the shade, covering the cut-outs.

Use a glue stick on the outer edges.

The lampshade cover should fit snugly.

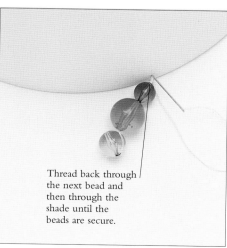

Thread the third bead and then put the needle back through the second bead.

Thread back through the next bead and then through the shade until the beads are secure.

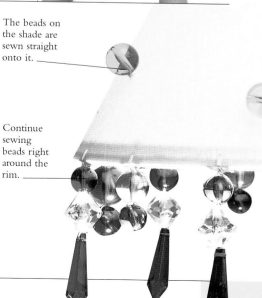

The beads on the shade are sewn straight onto it.

Continue sewing beads right around the rim.

Paper
POTS

Turn balloons into bowls with the art of papier mâché, and create some truly quirky containers. Award yourself a golden trophy, design a friendly face, or devise your own particular patterns and powerful prints with paper or paint.

1

Add a bit of abstract sculpture using egg box parts, or give yourself some star quality by attaching sequins and jewels. Keep the pots as empty ornaments, or use them to store small bits and pieces – anything from bangles to marbles, sweets to spare change.

2

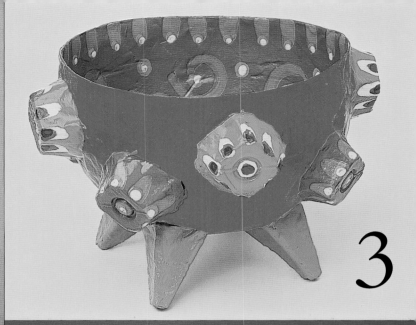

3

4

5

6

Paper Pots

Making a basic pot

Gather together the things you need, including balloons, petroleum jelly, newspaper, and wallpaper paste.

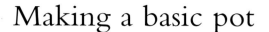

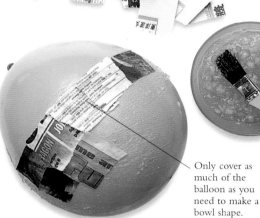

Only cover as much of the balloon as you need to make a bowl shape.

Sit the base of the balloon in a container to steady it while drying.

a) Blow up your balloon and tie it securely. Then spread a thin layer of petroleum jelly over the area you want to cover with paper.

b) Tear newspaper into pieces about 5 cm square. Brush wallpaper paste over the petroleum jelly and put the paper on in overlapping rows.

c) Brush paste over each layer before adding more paper. Add six layers, and leave to dry for two or three days. Then pull out, or burst, the balloon.

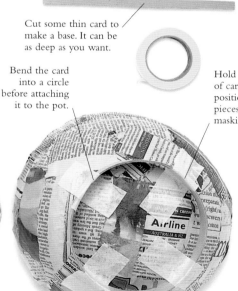

Use scissors to trim round the rim.

Cut some thin card to make a base. It can be as deep as you want.

Bend the card into a circle before attaching it to the pot.

Hold the circle of card in position with pieces of masking tape.

Pasted paper smooths out the base.

Smoothing out the rim

Trim off the ragged edge around the top of the pot. Paste squares of paper over the edge to smooth it over. Do this with three layers and leave to dry.

Making a base for your pot

The base of your pot can be made from a variety of things, such as yoghurt containers, toilet rolls, and discarded cartons. Or make your own by cutting a strip of thin card and making it into a band. Tape the base to the pot and cover it with three layers of paper and paste. Leave until completely dry.

Different colours will help enliven your design.

The base needs to be wide enough for the trophy to balance.

Making pot 1

To create the trophy, make handles out of card strips; add a tube for the stem; and use cartons to build the base. Tape and paste these to the pot. When the trophy is dry, cover it with gold acrylic paint and glue on a card laurel motif.

Making pot 2

Tear comics and magazines into strips to create colour and pattern. First paste strips onto the rim and base of your basic pot, then stick strips over the whole bowl, inside and out. Finish off with an acrylic varnish.

Keep the newspaper as smooth as possible.

If any glue oozes out, cover with more sequins.

Making pot 3

Alter the shape of your pot by adding pieces of egg carton to form legs or handles for the pot. Attach these to the pot with paste and paper. When everything is dry, paint the pot with acrylic paint and finish with varnish.

Making pot 4

Paint the pot with gold acrylic paint. Once it is dry, spread some PVA glue around the rim and roll the bowl through a pile of sequins and glitter. For extra sparkle, glue gems around the outside too.

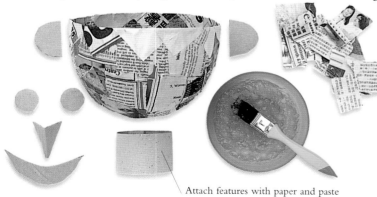

Attach features with paper and paste

The base colour should completely cover the newspaper.

Making pot 5

To make a face for the pot, cut out the features and neck from card and paste them to the pot with squares of paper. When the paste is dry, paint the whole pot with acrylic paint. Finish off with a coat of acrylic varnish.

Making pot 6

Use acrylic paint to decorate this pot. Paint the base colours on first – you can use orange inside and white outside. Paint the black stripes on afterwards. Finish off with a coat of acrylic varnish.

HANG Ups

Add character to your wardrobe by **creating** some humorous hang-ups. Your clothes will never look the same once they are draped over the shoulders of mixed-up **models**, anxious **aliens**, or mad, masked **animals**. Make the base, and then do **your own thing.**

Use cut-outs from magazines to stick over one another and create an abstract face.

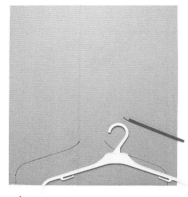

a) Lay a hanger on stiff cardboard and draw around it to make the shoulders and neck.

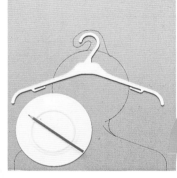

b) Draw around a small plate for the head, adding a thickened hook from the top of the hanger.

c) Cut out the whole shape with a craft knife. Remember to cut on a rubber mat.

d) Use cut-outs of facial features from magazines to build up into a crazy fashion victim.

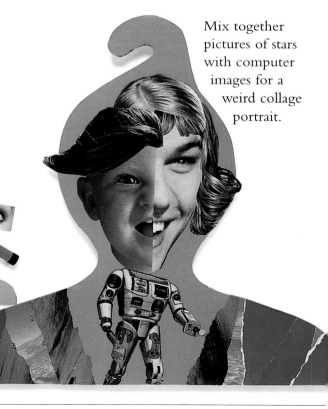

Mix together pictures of stars with computer images for a weird collage portrait.

Stick a different
shape over the face of
the hanger; paint it green; and
give it huge eyes for an alien
encounter.

Each distorted glamour girl will
be different when you create a
collage of caricatured features.

Once you've
painted on fur
patterns, attach
masks to make
dramatic heads
for animal
hangers – they're a
little spooky, too.

For simple
silliness, just
paint your
hanger and glue
on a pair of
joke glasses.

Collection BOXES

Forget the free gift inside your box of cereal; what about the box itself? With imaginative painting or wacky wrapping you can transform a cereal box into a set of display shelves to show off your favourite selection of souvenirs. Choose colours to complement your collections, or camouflage the box with anything from comics to wrapping paper or maps. Smaller boxes can be added on, or slotted in to make a drawer.

1

2

3

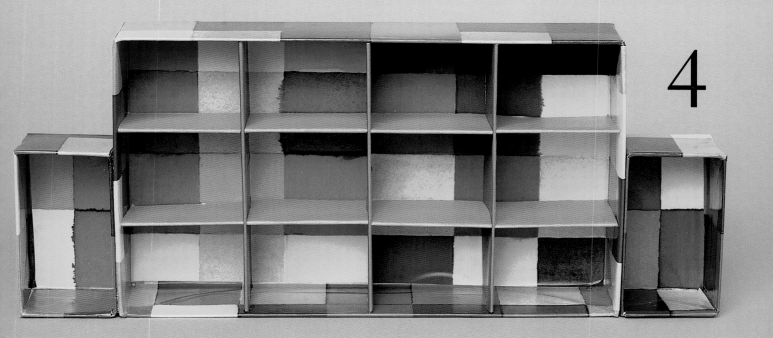

4

Collection Boxes

Making a basic box

Draw the X from corner to corner.

Cut from the centre outwards.

Gluing down the sides reinforces the box.

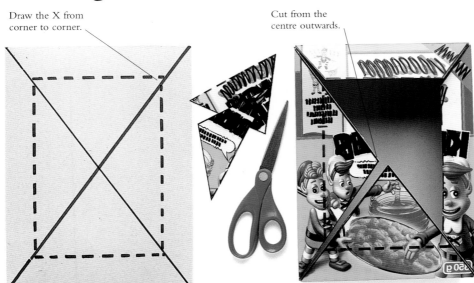

a) Mark an X across an empty cereal box. Measure the depth of the box. Draw a border that is the same width as the box's depth.

b) Cut along the X lines to open up the centre of the box. Cut away the centre panel – you will be left with a flap on each side.

c) Fold the flaps neatly down inside the box and glue them into position. Hold them in place until they are completely dry.

Use another cereal box to make the dividers.

Slits should be half the width of the dividers.

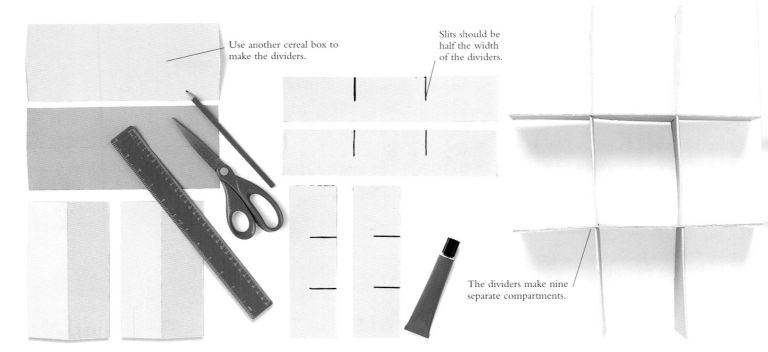

The dividers make nine separate compartments.

d) For the shelves, make dividers that run the height and width of the box. For extra strength, cut them twice as wide as the depth of the box.

e) Fold the pieces of card over and glue them down. They must be slotted together to go in the box, so mark the intersections and cut the slits.

f) Paint the dividers and then slot them together. Paint or wrap the box. Glue the back and side edges of the dividers and push them into the box.

Adding a drawer

You can make a drawer with card from another cereal box. However, an easier method is to use a smaller box that fits the width of a shelf compartment. Measure how high the drawer should be; then use scissors to cut off the top.

Make sure everything fits before you start decorating.

Mark the height of the drawer on all four sides of the box before you begin cutting.

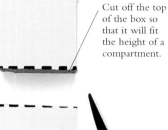

Cut off the top of the box so that it will fit the height of a compartment.

Attach a paper fastener as a handle.

Making box 1

The gold paint, combined with the flourish of decoration at the top of this box, gives it a theatrical feel. First make a basic box including a drawer. Then add the top decoration by cutting out your preferred shape from a cereal box. Allow enough width to make folds at the sides. Glue the decoration in place. Decide what you want to display, and then pick out your colour scheme to complement the dominant colours of your collection.

Paint the whole box before attaching decoration.

Mix PVA glue with the paint so the colour covers the card more effectively.

Paint the dividers before you put them in the box.

Making box 2

Boxes can be customized to fit particular objects. In this case, the toy cars are long and low, so you can make narrow compartments with your dividers to fit the car shapes. Add to the theme in your decoration by covering the box with an old road map. Paint the shelves and top panel with an acrylic paint and PVA mix before you stick the whole thing together.

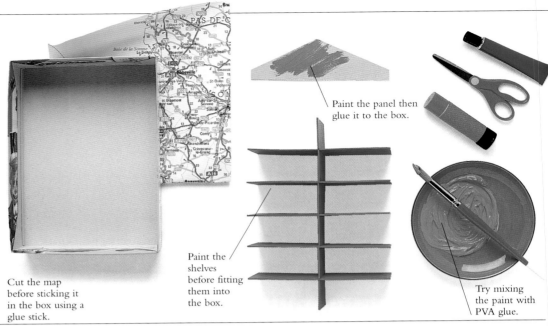

Cut the map before sticking it in the box using a glue stick.

Paint the shelves before fitting them into the box.

Paint the panel then glue it to the box.

Try mixing the paint with PVA glue.

Making box 3

For instant colour you can cover the boxes with pages from magazines or comics. Stick the paper to the box with a glue stick; then cover the dividers in the same way. Add a drawer that is also covered. Try to choose your pictures carefully, so that the compartments and drawer each have a dramatic central image.

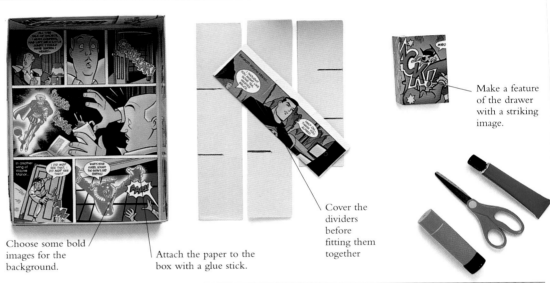

Choose some bold images for the background.

Attach the paper to the box with a glue stick.

Cover the dividers before fitting them together

Make a feature of the drawer with a striking image.

Making box 4

To extend the capacity of your box, try gluing an extra box on each side. Prepare the small boxes in the same way as the large cereal box by cutting out the front panel and making flaps that reinforce the sides. Paint the small boxes to match the larger one – or cover them with the same paper. Paint the dividers in contrasting colours, fit the slots together, and glue them into position.

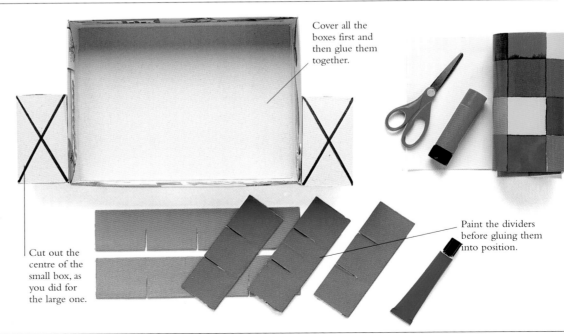

Cover all the boxes first and then glue them together.

Cut out the centre of the small box, as you did for the large one.

Paint the dividers before gluing them into position.

Making a magazine box

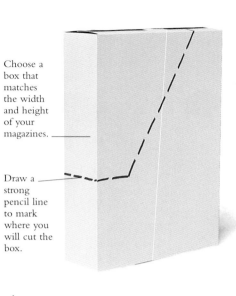

Choose a box that matches the width and height of your magazines.

Draw a strong pencil line to mark where you will cut the box.

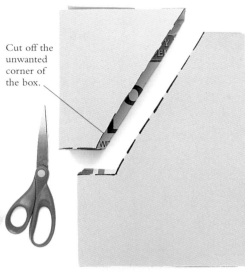

Cut off the unwanted corner of the box.

Cover the box in wrapping paper. Trim paper before folding it over the edges.

a) Draw lines on the box to mark where you need to cut off one of the corners to create an opening.

b) Using kitchen scissors, cut all the way round the lines including the top of the box.

c) Wrap the box in paper, trim the paper, and tape it down inside and underneath.

Odd boxes

You can change different size shoe boxes into a co-ordinated set of storage containers just by covering them in wrapping paper. Choose complementary colours and patterns or designs that highlight other colour schemes in your room.

Using ordinary gift wrapping paper, cover the boxes in matching or contrasting colours.

You can use the finished box for magazines, concert programmes, tall books, school files, or even stray pieces of paper.

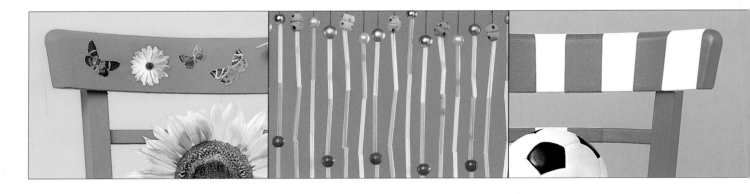

Index

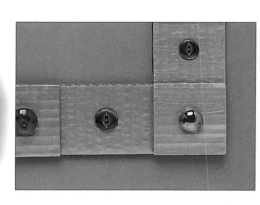